sea creatures

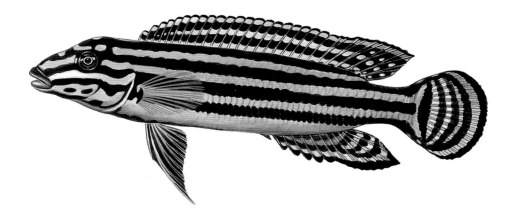

This edition published by Fog City Press
Conceived and produced by Weldon Owen Pty Ltd
61 Victoria Street, McMahons Point
Sydney, NSW 2060, Australia

Group Chief Executive Officer John Owen
President and Chief Executive Officer Terry Newell
Publisher Sheena Coupe
Creative Director Sue Burk
Vice President, International Sales Stuart Laurence
Vice President, Sales and New Business Development Amy Kaneko
Vice President, Sales: Asia and Latin America Dawn Low
Administrator, International Sales Kristine Ravn
Publishing Coordinator Mike Crowton

Consultant Editor Denise Ryan
Managing Editor Jessica Cox
Editor Helen Flint
Designer Gabrielle Green

ISBN: 978-1-74089-665-8

Color reproduction by SC (Sang Choy) International Pte Ltd
Printed by SNP Leefung Printers Ltd
Manufactured in China

10 9 8 7 6 5 4 3 2 1

A WELDON OWEN PRODUCTION

visual encyclopedia of

sea creatures

Robert Coupe

FOG CITY PRESS

Fish

Tube worms

contents

Gulper eel

What is a sea creature?

Some animals, such as whales and many fish, spend all their lives in the sea. Some fish, such as salmon, move between seas and rivers. Other animals, such as penguins and seals, live on land but find their food in the sea. All these animals are sea creatures.

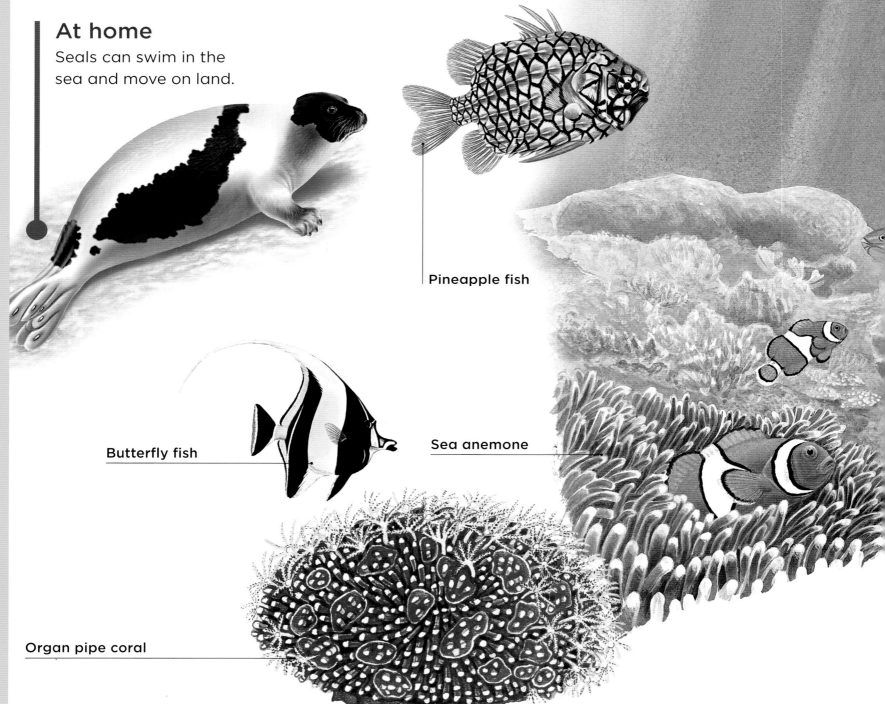

At home
Seals can swim in the sea and move on land.

Pineapple fish

Butterfly fish

Sea anemone

Organ pipe coral

All shapes and sizes

Creatures of all shapes and sizes live in the sea. Gray reef sharks swim and hunt in the open ocean, while brightly colored small fish live among coral reefs.

There are more than 24,000 different kinds of fish.

Octopus

7

Fish

Fish live in all the world's seas. They range from huge sharks to tiny creatures less than half-an-inch long. They have scales on their bodies, and use their side and tail fins to move through the water. They breathe through gills on the sides of their heads.

Malawi fish

Eye

Barbel
Fish use barbels to find food.

Gills
Fish use gills to breathe.

Side fin

Striped Julie

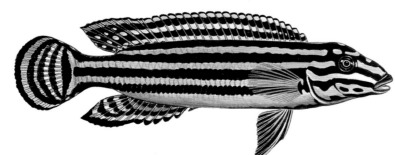

Spinecheek anemone fish

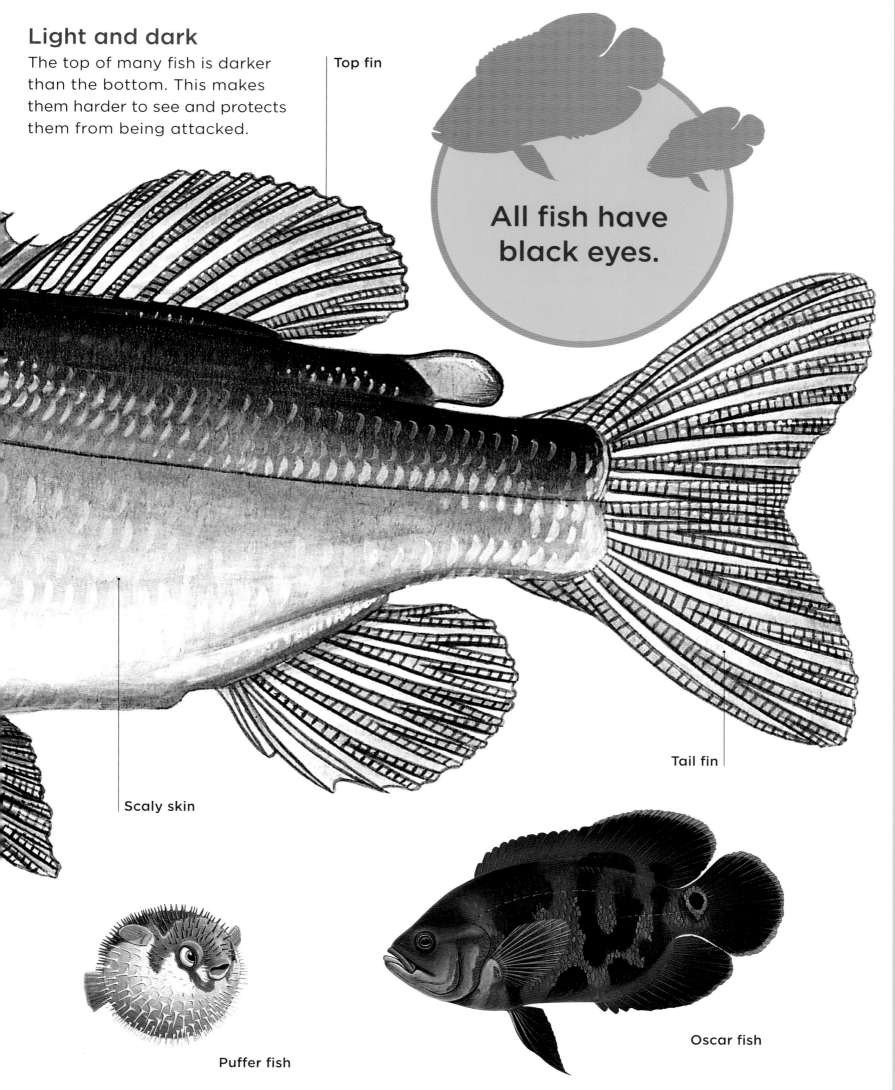

Light and dark

The top of many fish is darker than the bottom. This makes them harder to see and protects them from being attacked.

Top fin

All fish have black eyes.

Tail fin

Scaly skin

Puffer fish

Oscar fish

Sharks

There are about 350 kinds of sharks. All of them eat other fish and other sea creatures, but most will not harm humans. Many sharks use their strong tails to move quickly through the water. The whale shark can grow to 40 feet (12 m) in length and is the largest of all sharks.

INTO THE SEA

People who study great white and other dangerous sharks sometimes go under the sea in strong metal cages that the sharks cannot bite through.

Cage
Sharks cannot bite through the cage.

Shark

Slow swimmers

Port Jackson sharks live near the coast of southern Australia. They are slow swimmers, but they travel long distances every summer and winter.

Danger!

Great white sharks live in shallow waters near to coasts. They sometimes attack people. They have strong jaws and their mouths are filled with very sharp teeth.

Great white shark

Big teeth

Rays

Rays are fish that are close relatives of sharks. Their bodies are wide and flat and they have long, thin tails. They all have side fins that look similar to the wings of bats. There are six main types of rays.

When rays swim, they flap their side fins like the wings of a bird.

A sting in its tail

This stingray may look friendly, but a long spike at the tip of its tail can give a poisonous sting.

TWO FACES

A ray may seem to have two faces. Its eyes are on top of its head and its mouth and nostrils are underneath.

Nostril

Mouth

Electric fish

Torpedo rays catch the fish they eat by giving them an electric shock. They have organs behind their eyes that make electricity.

Mighty mouth

Most rays feed on the seafloor, but manta rays swim near the surface. As they move, masses of tiny plants and animals called plankton flow into their mouths.

Side fin

No danger
Though they are huge, manta rays are not dangerous to humans.

13

Whales

Whales are mammals, just like you and me. Female whales feed their babies on milk from their bodies. Whales have strong tails that they use to push themselves through the water. Many whales travel long distances across the world's oceans.

NO TEETH

Instead of teeth, some whales, such as bowhead whales, have long strips of baleen. This traps tiny plankton for them to eat.

Baleen

Whale tails

Fish tails move from side to side. Whale tails move up and down. Some whales slap their tails on the surface of the sea.

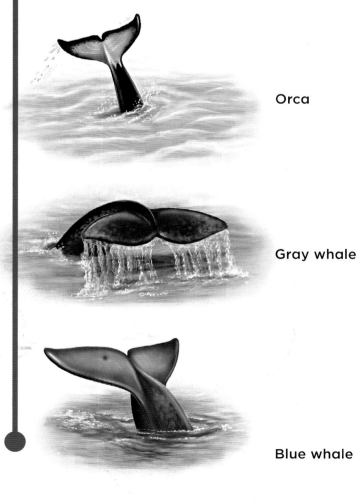

Orca

Gray whale

Blue whale

Holding their breath

Whales rise to the surface to breathe air through a hole in their heads, called a blowhole. But they can stay under the water without breathing for a long time.

Gray whale

Sei whale

The blue whale is the biggest animal anywhere in the world.

Orca

Dolphins and porpoises

You may have seen dolphins doing tricks at the zoo, or swimming, leaping, and diving near a beach. There are almost 40 kinds of dolphins, and some of them grow very large. Porpoises are generally smaller than dolphins and there are only six known kinds.

Fins

Porpoises use their backfin to help them swim. The finless porpoise is the only porpoise that does not have a fin on its back.

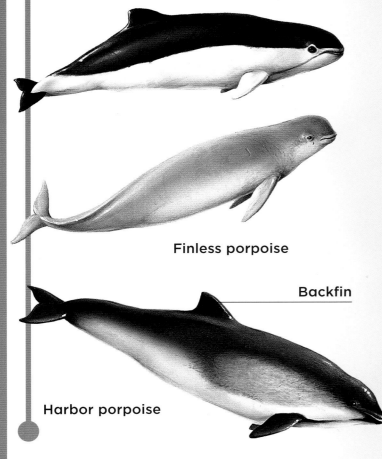

Spectacled porpoise

Finless porpoise

Backfin

Harbor porpoise

High jumps

Some dolphins jump high into the air. They do this when they are playing, but sometimes it is to tell other dolphins there are fish nearby.

Angry dolphins clap their jaws together and make whistling sounds.

Look alike

Dolphins that are closely related, like this mother and her calf, often look very much like each other.

Seals and sea lions

Adult sea lion

Seals are mammals, like whales and dolphins. However, seals spend much of their time on land and can move along the ground. Some seals have ears that you can see. They are sea lions. Other seals have ears that you cannot see.

Swimming for food

Sea lions, such as the ones here, swim in the sea to catch the fish and other sea creatures that they eat.

Flipper

Young sea lions can swim a month after they are born.

Fish

Pup

Tusks for digging

Walruses are close relatives of seals. They use their long tusks to dig crabs and shellfish from between rocks.

Penguins

Penguins are birds that do not fly. But they are good swimmers and divers. Most of them live in the cold southern parts of the world. Some penguins spend most of the time in the water. They hunt for fish and other sea animals.

Penguin diving

The smallest penguin, the little penguin, is smaller than a chicken.

Diving deep

Penguins can dive deep under the water. When they swim, they flap their wings, just like birds that fly in the air.

Emperor penguins

Emperor penguins are the largest penguins of all. They grow to 4 feet (1.2 m) in height. They live in Antarctica all year round.

Snares penguin

Snares penguins live on a small island off the south coast of New Zealand. They have a small white patch on each cheek.

King penguin

Octopuses and squid

Octopuses have eight arms, called tentacles. There are suckers on the tentacles that catch food. Squid are like octopuses. They have ten arms, which also have suckers for catching food. Some squid and octopuses are tiny. Some are huge.

Tiny but dangerous

The blue-ringed octopus is only as big as a golf ball, but it is highly poisonous.

COLOR CHANGE

An octopus can change color quickly. It can make itself look like part of a rock or like sand.

Squid

Ink

Squirting ink

When a shark or other animal attacks a squid, the squid can squirt a cloud of black ink from inside its body.

Frill shark

The giant squid can grow to the size of a bus.

Jewels of the sea

Many sea creatures live deep in the ocean where it is too dark to see any color. But in the warm, shallow waters of tropical areas, colorful coral reefs grow like huge underwater gardens. Brightly colored fish, shellfish, turtles, worms, and other creatures live among coral reefs.

Sea stars

We sometimes call sea stars starfish, but they are not fish. They have soft bodies and five arms that stick out like the points of a star.

SHELL HOMES

Many small sea creatures have shells that cover their bodies and help protect them from other animals.

Coral reefs

Most coral reefs are in the Pacific and Indian oceans. More than 3,000 different types of fish live on reefs in the Indian Ocean.

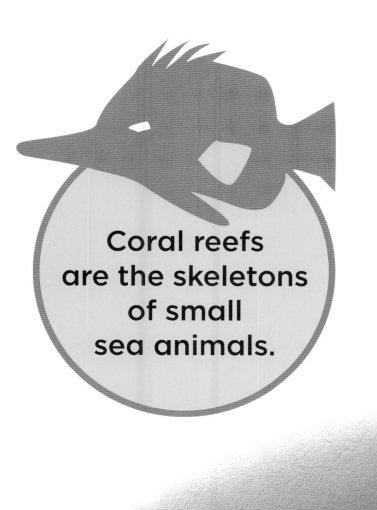

Coral reefs are the skeletons of small sea animals.

Jellyfish

The bodies of jellyfish look like bells. Underneath they have long arms, or tentacles, which they use to catch small animals.

Part-timers

There are animals that live on the land or fly in the air that never move far from the seas and oceans. This is because the sea is where they find their food. Many kinds of birds eat only fish. Polar bears often grab seals from the freezing polar waters.

Hungry bear

Polar bears are fierce hunters, especially when food is hard to find. This one has broken through ice to catch a baby beluga whale.

Hot and cold

Marine iguanas are the only lizards that live in the sea. They bask on rocks in the sun to warm up.

Marine iguanas sneeze out the salt they get from seawater.

Baby beluga whale

FLYING WITH FISH

Ospreys are birds that eat only fish. They catch the fish in their strong claws and carry them away to eat them.

Near the surface

Plankton is the name we use for the millions of tiny animals and plants that float in the sunlight on the sea's surface. Small fish and other small sea animals feed on plankton. Salmon and other larger fish then eat the small fish.

Hunters and hunted

An orca, or killer whale, chases a seal, while a salmon swims after a school of herring not far below the sea's surface.

Young salmon live in rivers. Adult salmon swim to the sea.

28

On coral reefs

Large schools of squirrelfish swim through coral reefs in the shallow tropical waters of the Pacific and Indian oceans.

IN AND OUT

Turtles can live in and out of the water. Many lobsters spend their lives under the water, in shallow coastal seas.

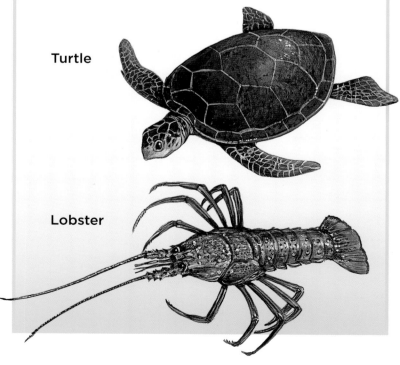

Turtle

Lobster

In the deep

Deep down in the sea, where the sunlight does not reach, it is very dark. Many sea creatures such as fish, squid, eels, and jellyfish, spend their lives in the ocean depths. Most deep-sea creatures never come to the surface.

Submarine

A big gulp

This black gulper eel has huge jaws, very small teeth, a tiny eye, and a long tail that gets thinner and thinner toward the end.

Hatchet fish

Gulper eel

Tube worms

At one end, giant white tube worms are stuck to the seabed. At the other end, they have bright red breathing organs.

Tube worm

Big and small

The world's biggest animal, the blue whale, lives in the sea. So do plankton, which are some of the world's tiniest creatures. Plankton are so small you cannot see them. They are the main food for some of the largest whales and sharks.

No harm
This whale shark has no teeth and cannot harm people.

Whale shark

Big fish

The whale shark is not only the biggest of all sharks; it is also the biggest of all fish. It feeds mainly on plankton and small fish.

Great white shark

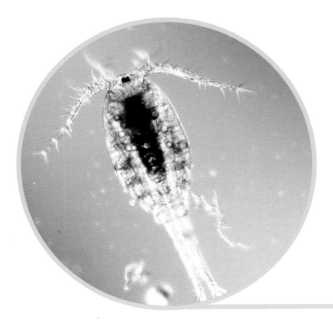

Krill are tiny sea creatures that look like shrimp. Many whales, seals, and seabirds eat krill.

The world's smallest fish grows less than half an inch (1 cm) long.

Black marlin

Wels catfish

Barracuda

Green moray

Footballer cod

Blackfin pacu

Bigeye

Blue tang

Clownfish

Great hunters

Most sea creatures hunt other animals. Some eat only one kind of fish or animal. Others eat different types of food. In most cases, larger animals hunt for smaller animals. Some animals hunt alone. Others search for food in groups or in large packs.

The orca is one of the fastest creatures in the sea.

Deadly tail

The tail of the thresher shark is like a long whip. The shark uses its tail to trap fish and then beat them to death.

Tail

Killer whales

Orcas, or killer whales, are clever hunters. Sometimes an orca will lunge onto a beach and frighten seals into the water, where other orcas catch and eat them.

Protection

Different animals have different ways of protecting themselves against attack. Some fish have bright colors, stripes, or spots that make them hard to see. Other sea creatures have to fight back to save themselves from being caught and eaten.

Puffing up

Puffer fish can puff up their bodies until they are too large for other fish to swallow. Their bodies also contain a strong poison.

Circle of tails

Sperm whales form a circle around their young when orcas attack them. They slap the water hard with their tails to frighten the orcas away.

SWORD FIGHT

Narwhals are whales with long tusks that are similar to swords. Male narwhals use these tusks to defend themselves and to fight each other over females.

Clownfish live among the stinging tentacles of sea anemones to stay safe.

Fantastic journeys

Some sea creatures make long journeys every year. We call these journeys "migrations." Some whales travel from warm parts of the world to cold polar waters. Here they eat the huge amounts of krill that they need to survive for the rest of the year.

Gray whales swim from Mexico to Alaska, USA, and back every year.

Around the world
Arctic terns fly from the North Pole to the South Pole. Some of them fly around Antarctica before they make the return journey.

LONG-DISTANCE SWIMMERS

Sockeye salmon hatch into rivers. They then swim from here into the ocean. They return to the rivers to lay their eggs.

Female turtle

Baby turtle

Traveling turtles

Sea turtles spend a long time building up stores of fat. They need these stores so they can travel across the oceans to areas where they lay their eggs.

Next generation

Most baby fish hatch from eggs. At first they are tiny creatures, called larvae. They swim freely in the ocean until they grow into adults. Other sea creatures, such as whales, give birth to babies that are fully formed and ready to swim.

Mother humpback whale

FIRST BREATH

As soon as an Irrawaddy dolphin is born, its mother takes it to the surface to get its first breath of air.

Humpback calf

Mother and child

When it is born, a baby humpback whale is about one-third the size of its mother. It grows quickly by sucking milk from its mother's body.

All baby clownfish are born male. Some turn into females later in life.

Legends of the sea

In days gone by, long sea journeys were very dangerous. So it is not surprising that sailors made up stories featuring imaginary sea monsters. Some of these monsters are similar to sea creatures that really exist.

Kraken tentacle

Kraken

In Norway, people told stories about a creature similar to a giant octopus. It was called a kraken. It could hold a ship in its huge tentacles.

Scary beasts

The animals below are imaginary creatures. However, there are some real sea animals that look a bit like them.

Looking after the sea

The oceans are home to millions of sea creatures. However, people use the oceans, too. They swim in them, fish them, and sail ships across them. Some of the things that people do can harm the oceans and the creatures that live there.

Oil that spills from big ships can kill or injure sea animals, such as this sea otter.

Trapped by mistake

Fishing nets often catch the wrong kinds of sea animals. Dolphins and sharks that get caught in these nets can be injured or killed.

WHALE PRODUCTS

Whales were once killed for their oil. This oil was used for many things, including face creams and candles.

In the last few years almost 100 kinds of fish have died out.

Trapped hammerhead shark

Old fishing net

Glossary

Coral

Seal

Antarctica

The continent of land, ice, and snow that surrounds the South Pole

arctic

The region near Earth's North Pole

baleen

Long strips of an elastic-like substance in the mouths of some kinds of whales

beluga

A white whale with a large, round head that lives in seas near the North Pole

coral

A colored substance, formed from the skeletons of tiny sea creatures called coral polyps

crustacean

A sea creature with a hard outer shell

Equator

The imaginary line around Earth that divides the top half from the bottom

gills

Organs on the side of a fish's head through which it breathes oxygen

iguana

A type of large lizard that is found mainly in South America

krill

Tiny sea creatures that are similar to shrimp

larvae

Small wormlike creatures that hatch from the eggs of insects and some fish

mammal

An animal whose young feed on their mother's milk

Clownfish

Arctic tern

migration

The long journey that many animals, such as birds, whales, and some fish, make from one part of Earth to another

mollusks

A sea creature with a soft body and a hard shell

ocean

A large area of seawater on Earth's surface. There are five oceans on Earth.

orca

A large black and white dolphin that hunts penguins, fish, and seals

plankton

Tiny plants or animals that float or swim slowly through the water

polar

Areas near Earth's North and South poles

reef

A line of rocks or coral near the surface of the water

suckers

Parts of the tentacles of an octopus that stick onto fish and other sea creatures

tentacles

The long, thin outer parts of octopuses and some other sea creatures

tropical

Of the tropics, which are the warm parts of Earth near the Equator

Index

Credits

Key t=top; l=left; r=right; tl=top left; tcl=top center left; tc=top center; tcr=top center right; tr=top right; cl=center left; c=center; cr=center right; b=bottom; bl=bottom left; bcl=bottom center left; bc=bottom center; bcr=bottom center right; br=bottom right

Photographs
COR=Corel Corp; iS=istockphoto.com; PD=Photodisc; PL=photolibrary.com

12c iS **19**tr PD **21**tr COR **22**tr iS **24**bl iS **25**tr iS **29**bl COR **32**bl PL **36**tr COR **44**cl PD

Illustrations
Front cover Trevor Ruth c, Rob Mancini tr; David Kirshner cr, Tony Pyrakowski/Alistar Barnard/Frank Knight br
Back cover Simone End tr, Christer Eriksson br

Jane Beatson **27**br; Ann Bowman **38**cr, **47**tr, **12**br c; Marjorie Crosby Fairall **29**br; Marc Dando/The Art Agency **22**bl; Simone End **18**c t, **30**tr; Christer Eriksson **10**c, **26**bl tr, **32**r, **40**c; Ray Grinaway **44**c; David Kirshner **1**c, **3**c, **4**tl, **5**tr, **6**c, **8**bl br c tr, **9**br, **11**tr, **14**bl c, **30**l, **40**bl, **32**cr, **38**b, **47**tl; Frank Knight, **9**bl; Trevor Ruth **4**bl, **38**tr; P. Scott/The Art Agency **20**c; Rod Scott **28**c, **40**c; Mark Stewart/The Art Agency **25**br; Roger Swainston **6**c, **22**c, **24**c, **32**bl tr; Chris Turnbull/The Art Agency **10**bl; Glen Vause **44**bl; Magic Group **6**b, **21**br, **46**tl; The Art Agency **14**tr, **16**c, **17**br, **36**bc, **37**tr, **43**r